PARANORMAL HANDBOOKS

GHOSTS, POLTERGEISTS AND HAUNTED HOUSES

BY SEAN McCOLLUM

Raintree is an imprint of Capstone Global Library Limited, a company incorporated in England and Wales having its registered office at 264 Banbury Road, Oxford, OX2 7DY – Registered company number: 6695582

www.raintree.co.uk
myorders@raintree.co.uk

Text © Capstone Global Library Limited 2017
The moral rights of the proprietor have been asserted.

Edited by Nate LeBoutillier
Designed by Philippa Jenkins
Picture research by Svetlana Zhurkin
Production by Kathy McColley
Printed and bound in China

ISBN 978 1 4747 2405 0
20 19 18 17 16
10 9 8 7 6 5 4 3 2 1

British Library Cataloguing in Publication Data
A full catalogue record for this book is available from the British Library.

Acknowledgements
We would like to thank the following for permission to reproduce photographs: Alamy: Classic Image, 6, Pictorial Press, 23, Wallace Weeks, 18; AP Photo: Mark Humphrey, 16; Corbis: Bettmann, 20; Getty Images: The LIFE Picture Collection/David E. Scherman, 17; International Mapping, 28 (middle); Library of Congress, 9, 21, 22; Newscom: Album/Laika Entertainment, 10, Danita Delimont Photography/Walter Bibikow, 28 (top middle), Design Pics, 11, Europics, 26, Mirrorpix, 12; Shutterstock: Africa Studio, 8, Anastasia Tveretinova, 14 (top), Anki Hoglund, 27, Antlio, cover (bottom), 1, Arda Savasciogullari, 3, 29, Artistas, 14 (bottom), Darla Hallmark, 28 (top left), Dmitry Zimin, 5, Everett Collection, 24, karenfoley-photography, 28 (bottom right), katalinks, 7, KMcNamara, 28 (top right), Lario Tus, cover (top), back cover, Mariusz S. Jurgielewicz, 28 (bottom left), nutech21, 25, Zack Frank, 28 (bottom middle)
Every effort has been made to contact copyright holders of material reproduced in this book. Any omissions will be rectified in subsequent printings if notice is given to the publisher.

Design elements by Shutterstock.

CONTENTS

The vanishing hitch-hiker

A couple of friends are driving on a dark road on a cold night. They are surprised to see a shivering teenage girl. She is barefoot and not wearing a coat. They quickly pull over and pick her up.

The girl gets into the back seat and gives them the address where she lives. "My mother will be so worried," the girl says. They drive to an old house and pull onto the driveway. The driver glances in the rearview mirror and gasps. Both friends turn around. The back seat is empty. The girl has mysteriously disappeared!

Mystified, the friends go to the door and are met by an old woman. They explain what happened and describe the girl they had picked up. "That sounds like my daughter," the old woman says. "She was killed in a car accident 20 years ago, near where you picked her up."

This ghost story is known as "The Vanishing Hitch-hiker". Versions of it are told in many countries, including Korea, Japan and the United States. Some people will swear it's true, saying they know the friends it happened to.

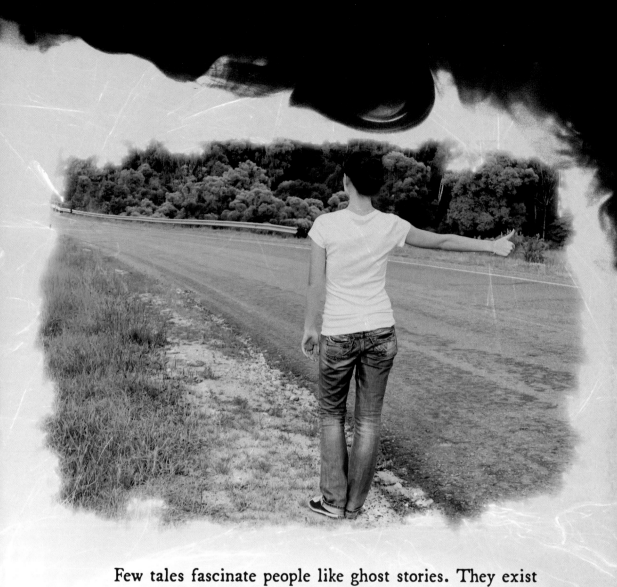

Few tales fascinate people like ghost stories. They exist in every culture. But do ghosts truly walk the Earth? Do they hitch-hike its roads? Science has not found any proof that spirits of the dead exist. But that does not mean they do not haunt our imaginations.

CHAPTER 1

THE MYSTERY OF GHOSTS

One of the oldest ghost stories we know of appears in *The Epic of Gilgamesh*. This ancient poem is more than 4,200 years old. In it, Gilgamesh and his fellow warrior Enkidu perform many heroic acts together. But after

Gilgamesh (right) helps Enkidu (left) best the Bull of Ishtar.

Enkidu dies, Gilgamesh seeks out his ghost in the underworld. With the help of two gods, the two friends are able to meet again.

The idea of ghosts is as old as human history. In most ghost stories, ghosts are spirits of dead people that appear to the living. At the heart of these tales is a very deep question: What happens to people when they die? Where do their feelings, memories and personalities go? Science offers few answers to these questions. Therefore many people turn to religion and myth to explore them.

FREAKY FACT
A 2013 poll found that 52 per cent of UK residents believe that ghosts exist.

Ghosts appear in many forms in legends and tales. Some ghosts are nasty and monstrous. Some "lost souls" are described as lonely and sad. Others are kind and helpful – or perhaps full of **mischief**. In many instances ghosts in these stories have unfinished tasks they want to complete. They may be inspired by true love, a wish to help others or hunger for revenge.

mischief playful behaviour causing harm or trouble

Historical ghosts

Reports of ghosts are often linked to historical events. Some spirits are said to be so heartbroken that they cannot leave the place where they died.

Queen Esther

In the mid-1700s, a battle took place in Pennsylvania, USA. It pitted a group of white soldiers against a village of Native Americans called the Iroquois. According to some sources, the Iroquois warriors had been responsible for the killing of some white settlers. After a fierce fight, the soldiers overran the village. Queen Esther, a young Iroquois leader, tried to get her people to safety. They were caught. According to one story, the soldiers forced Queen Esther to watch them drown all the women and children of her village. Then they **lynched** her.

Years after the massacre, settlers reported hearing screams in the forest. Hunters in the area have also told of seeing a weeping woman hanging from a tree branch – then she suddenly disappears.

lynch murder, often by hanging, by a mob

Ghosts of Gettysburg

In July 1863, a bloody battle of the US Civil War (1861–1865) took place near Gettysburg, Pennsylvania. Thousands of soldiers were killed or wounded there. Since then some visitors to the battleground have reported hearing shouts, screams and booms of distant cannons.

One hundred years after the war, two people claimed to have seen ghostly wounded soldiers being cared for in a building basement. The building had been a hospital during the battle.

Battle of Gettysburg

Famous ghosts in stories and films

Writers and film-makers have shared thousands of stories about ghosts. These portrayals contribute to our ideas about ghosts and other spirits.

ParaNorman was nominated for a Best Animated Feature Academy Award.

FRIENDLY AND FUNNY GHOSTS	
Ghostbusters (1984, 2016)	A team of scientists uses its wits to save New York City from a spirit invasion.
ParaNorman (2012)	An 11-year-old boy uses his ability to talk to the dead to save his town and right a past wrong.
Beetlejuice (1988)	Two married ghosts call up a wild and crazy spirit called Beetlejuice. He helps save them and their haunted home.

FREAKY FACT

In the past, corpses were often wrapped in shrouds of white cloth before burial. This helps explain drawings of ghosts that look like they are wearing a bed sheet.

William Shakespeare's *Hamlet* featured Hamlet's father (right) in ghost form.

VENGEFUL AND FRIGHTENING GHOSTS

Hamlet by William Shakespeare (about 1600)	Hamlet's father may be the most famous ghost in literature. Early in the play, the ghost of the former king tells his son that he was murdered. Hamlet then sets out to avenge his father's death.
A Christmas Carol by Charles Dickens (1843)	In this famous book, Ebenezer Scrooge starts out as a mean, lonely man. But a visit from the chain-rattling ghost of his former business partner helps scare Scrooge into changing his ways.
Monster House (2006)	A team of children discovers the secret of an evil house and works together to free spirits trapped there.

CHAPTER 2

POLTERGEISTS: TROUBLEMAKING SPIRITS

In 2006 a family in South Shields told of spooky goings-on in their home. Stuffed animals flew by themselves, hitting the family. Something seemed determined to yank the covers off the bed while they slept. Threatening messages appeared on their 3-year-old son's toys.

Poltergeists or stressed kids?

Some psychologists offer non-paranormal explanations for poltergeists. They note the activity often centres around one person in the home. Usually it is a child who is feeling especially unhappy or stressed. The child may be acting out his or her unhappiness by secretly causing trouble and doing damage. These children may have no memory of what they have done.

The family and **paranormal** researchers blamed the experience on a poltergeist. Poltergeist is a German term that means "noisy spirit". Unlike ghosts in ghost stories, poltergeists do not appear in visible form. Some ghost experts do not consider them ghosts at all.

Poltergeists are mainly mischief-makers. They are said to **inhabit** homes where they knock ornaments off of shelves, throw objects and mess with the electrics. In extreme cases they have been accused of physically attacking victims.

Like ghosts, poltergeist activity has never been confirmed as a **supernatural** event. But stories about poltergeists often appear on the internet. Some people even share online videos that supposedly show poltergeists behaving badly.

paranormal something with no scientific explanation
inhabit live in
supernatural something that cannot be given an ordinary explanation

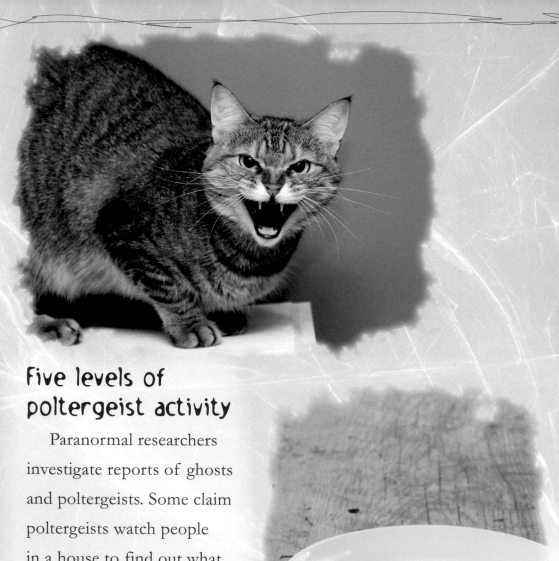

Five levels of poltergeist activity

Paranormal researchers investigate reports of ghosts and poltergeists. Some claim poltergeists watch people in a house to find out what scares them most.

The spirit's activity is said to grow more intense and dangerous as time passes. Researchers have divided the activity into five levels.

14

LEVEL 1
Getting noticed

Pets may react badly. People may hear odd noises, smell strange odours, feel unexplained cold spots in the house. They may sense that they are being watched.

LEVEL 2
Leaving physical signs

People may hear moaning. They may also feel breezes circulating in closed rooms.

LEVEL 3
Acting annoying

Lights and electrics may turn on or off by themselves. People may feel like they are being touched or pushed.

LEVEL 4
Moving and smashing

Furniture moves or shakes for no reason. Plates and other objects are smashed. Loud voices come from nowhere.

LEVEL 5
Attacking

Victims are scratched, bitten or slapped by unseen forces. They may be struck by flying objects. The poltergeist is sometimes accused of leaving threatening notes.

Famous poltergeist cases

The Bell Witch

The legend of the Bell Witch took place in Tennessee, USA, from 1817-1821. According to accounts, the spirit pounded on walls of the Bell family home. It threw objects, spoke out loud, shook hands, and pinched and slapped people. Though the being was described as a "witch", it behaved like a poltergeist.

Carney Bell, a descendent of John Bell, posed with a Bell Witch informational sign in Tennessee, USA.

The "Danny" Poltergeist Case

In the 1990s an alleged poltergeist event occurred in Georgia, USA. The Cobb family bought an antique bed for their 14-year-old son, Jason. The bed seemed to come with a poltergeist, they later told investigators. An unseen force began moving and throwing objects, flipping chairs and leaving notes. One note told who the spirit was: "Danny, 7". Another note explained that Danny's mother had died in the bed in 1899.

The Borley Rectory poltergeist hoax

In the 1930s, Borley Rectory was considered the most haunted place in England. There were many reported incidents of unexplained activity there. These included the mysterious ringing of servant bells and a "magic" self-playing piano. Famous writers and investigators visited. They went away convinced a poltergeist was at work.

Years later, children who had lived in the house confessed it was all a **hoax**. They described how they rigged the bells, the piano and other parts of the house to trick visitors into thinking it was haunted. Some people, however, are still convinced that it was a poltergeist's mischief.

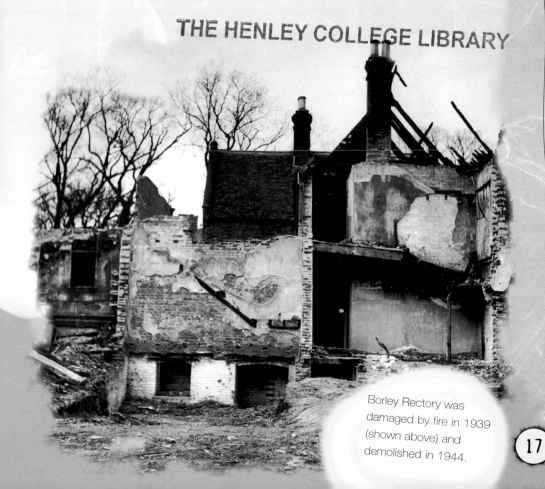

Borley Rectory was damaged by fire in 1939 (shown above) and demolished in 1944.

Infamous haunted houses in America

Wherever you live, somewhere near by is likely to be haunted. It might be a graveyard. It might be an old farmhouse. It might even be the home of an important politician.

The house in Amityville

Amityville is a quiet village on Long Island, New York, USA. In 1974 a horrible crime happened in a house there. A man shot and killed six members of his family.

A year later, another family moved into that same house. Family members reported experiencing a series of very scary events. The mother was lifted off her bed and left floating in the air. They said they saw visions of creatures,

the house in Amityville

including a demon-like pig. Green slime oozed from walls and the keyhole in the children's playroom. The family moved out after only 28 days. Their story is told in the book *The Amityville Horror*.

White House hauntings?

The White House, home of the US president, has stood for more than 200 years. It is easy to imagine famous people walking its historic corridors. The ghosts of several are said to still haunt the house, including Abraham Lincoln. Visitors also tell of seeing Abigail Adams, the wife of President John Adams, hanging laundry.

Former US President Abraham Lincoln

Myrtles Plantation

Myrtles Plantation in Louisiana, USA, has been called the most haunted house in America. Several murders took place there in the past. One man was shot and died on the main staircase of the house. Today the place is a bed and breakfast hotel. Guests and employees say they have heard the ghost of the dying man crawling up the stairs. Other ghostly experiences are commonly reported as well.

FREAKY FACT

Some houses that are said to be haunted can be difficult to sell. Occasionally, though, houses sell *more* quickly because of reported paranormal activity. Many online sites keep track of reportedly haunted houses.

Other haunted places

Haunted houses are not the only places where ghosts are supposedly spotted. Ghostly sightings are also common in ships, theatres and abandoned buildings.

The USS *Constellation*

The USS *Constellation* was one of the first warships ever built for the US Navy. It was launched in 1797 and saw action in several wars. Today the restored ship is a floating museum in Maryland, USA. One reported spirit is that of Thomas Truxton, the USS *Constellation's* first captain. An account says that his ghost even guided unsuspecting visitors on a tour of his old ship.

The USS *Constellation*

Theatre Royal, Drury Lane

Almost every playhouse has a ghost story. The Theatre Royal in London has been around since the 1600s. It is reportedly haunted by the "Man in Grey". He is described as a gentleman dressed in clothing from the 1700s. Witnesses sometimes report seeing him wandering among the seats. Another ghost

Joseph Grimaldi

there is said to be of the famous clown Joseph Grimaldi. Some anxious actors describe feeling his calming spirit while onstage.

Willard Asylum for the Chronically Insane

Asylums are notorious for being haunted. Willard Asylum for the Chronically Insane in New York, USA, was abandoned long ago. But visitors have reported seeing a ghostly red-headed patient there. She has been seen walking the corridors, letting out occasional midnight screams.

asylum hospital for people who are mentally ill

CHAPTER 4

PURSUING THE PARANORMAL

What would you want to know if you could talk to the dead? The question fascinates many who are interested in ghosts and spirits.

Seances and mediums

Curiosity about the afterlife leads some people to take part in **seances**. These meetings were especially popular in the 1800s. **Mediums** might go into a trance and then answer questions people had for dead relatives. Sometimes the ritual

seance meeting to contact the spirits of the dead
medium person who claims to make contact with spirits of the dead

included mysterious events such as floating tables or "spirit slates" on which supposed messages from the dead appeared.

The Fox sisters gained fame as mediums in the 1850s. Young Kate and Margaret asked questions. A spirit would supposedly answer "yes" or "no" by a number of knocks.

In 1888, Kate and Margaret confessed that they had completely faked their act. But by then their demonstrations had sparked a new religion called Spiritualism. Spiritualists believe that the living can communicate with the dead.

The popularity of seances eventually caught the attention of **sceptics**. In the 1880s a commission from the University of Pennsylvania launched an investigation. Every medium was found to be a fake. They used stage tricks to fool audiences and customers. Even so, mediums and psychics continue to make a living today by appealing to people hoping to contact the dead.

FREAKY FACT

Ouija boards first appeared in 1891 and are still popular today. Some people consider this "game" a way to communicate with ghosts and spirits.

sceptic person doubtful of paranormal events

a modern ghost hunter and his equipment

Ghost hunting today

The hobby of ghost hunting continues to grow. Several reality TV programmes about exploring haunted places have become popular.

Today's ghost hunters make a show of using high-tech gadgets. This electronic equipment often includes:

- hand-held devices that can detect changes in electromagnetic fields
- photographic and video cameras that use night-vision lenses
- infrared thermometers that can measure changes in room temperature
- digital recorders to capture mysterious noises and sounds

These devices look very professional. Ghost hunters claim they can pinpoint paranormal activity. However, there is no evidence that this is the case.

Almost all trained scientists consider paranormal investigation a **pseudoscience**. Chemistry, biology, physics and other scientific fields use experiments to prove or disprove an idea. Ghost hunting cannot do the same.

Without proof, why are we still so fascinated by ghosts? Perhaps we are very curious about what happens to people when they die. We want to know if the human spirit lives on after the heart beats for the last time. For that reason we will never stop exploring ghost stories – and trying to prove the existence of ghosts.

pseudoscience field of study that makes claims that cannot be proven

Haunted hot spots in the United States

Here are eight famous haunted sites in the United States.
They are worthy of more research.

VILLISCA AXE MURDER HOUSE,
Villisca, Iowa

THE STANLEY HOTEL,
Estes Park, Colorado

THE LINCOLN THEATER,
Decatur, Illinois

THE OHIO STATE REFORMATORY,
Mansfield, Ohio

EASTERN STATE PENITENTIARY,
Philadelphia, Pennsylvania

MISSION SAN MIGUEL,
San Luis Obispo, California

ST. LOUIS CEMETERY,
New Orleans, Louisiana

TRANS-ALLEGHENY LUNATIC ASYLUM,
West Virginia

HANDBOOK QUIZ

1. What contributes a lot to our ideas about ghosts and other spirits?

a. scientific research
b. stories and films
c. historical reports
d. personal experience

2. How are poltergeists different from ghosts?

a. Ghosts are more dangerous than poltergeists.
b. Ghosts are noisier than poltergeists.
c. Poltergeists don't appear in visible form, but ghosts do.
d. Poltergeists are not real but ghosts are.

3. What do places that are reportedly haunted often have in common?

a. They have a history of violence, murder or misery.
b. They are very old.
c. They have been abandoned and are now empty.
d. Dead bodies have been found there.

4. What do seances and mediums try to do?

a. find scientific proof of ghosts and other spirits
b. communicate with spirits of the dead
c. join the religion of Spiritualism
d. entertain people with stage magic

5. Why do most scientists consider ghost hunting a pseudoscience?

a. Ghost hunters are well-trained.
b. Anyone can claim to be a ghost hunter.
c. Ghost hunters have high-tech equipment, like real scientists.
d. It is impossible for ghost hunters to prove that ghosts exist.

Answers: 1-b, 2-c, 3-a, 4-b, 5-d

GLOSSARY

asylum hospital for people who are mentally ill

hoax trick to make people believe something that is not true

inhabit live in

lynch murder, often by hanging, by a mob

medium person who claims to make contact with spirits of the dead

mischief playful behaviour causing harm or trouble

paranormal something that has no scientific explanation

pseudoscience field of study that makes claims that cannot be proven

seance meeting to contact the spirits of the dead

sceptic person doubtful of paranormal events

supernatural something that cannot be given an ordinary explanation

READ MORE

Non-fiction

Ghosts (Usborne True Strories), Paul Dowswell and Tony Allan (Usborne Publishing, 2008)

Ghosts and Hauntings (Solving Mysteries with Science), Jane Bingham (Raintree, 2013)

Tracking Ghosts (Spooked), Emily Raij (Raintree, 2015)

Fiction

A Christmas Carol (Puffin Classics), Charles Dickens (Puffin Classics, 2008)

The Legend of Sleepy Hollow (Graphic Revolve), retold by Blake A Hoena (Raintree, 2011)

Stories from Shakespeare, Geraldine McCaughrean (Orion Children's Books, 2001)

INDEX